BREAKING FREE

Breaking Free by Sharon Raymond

Published 2016

ISBN 978 0 9569 448 7 0

A selection of Christian Verse inspired by God

Illustrations — Eva Jackson & Sharon Raymond

Front cover — Paul Clark

This book is dedicated to God, and my mum who never got to read it. With special thanks to my husband Michael, my Dad and all my family and friends who encouraged me to write this book, and to Eva for her amazing illustrations.

Content   Page

Forward

If someone had told me 18 months ago that I would write a book of verse I would have laughed! I am not a writer and the thought of putting feelings down on paper was my worst nightmare, but God had other ideas.

New Wine 2014, Michael (my husband) and I were working in the Bible Society Cafe. Working was the only way that I would attend New Wine — I didn't like crowds of people and my last experience at New Wine had not been very good. We attended the main sessions in the marquee when we weren't working. These were always crowded events, so not my idea of fun! Most times I would go into the tent trying to find a way to get out. During one of the evening sessions the Lord gave me a word which I felt should be given to the leadership. I wanted to take it forward but there were too many people, so I asked my friend if he would take it. He said no, but he would go forward with me. We tried three times to get through but there were just so many people. We eventually managed to find Mark Bailey and I handed the word across. We then made our way back to our seat; by the time I got back I was shaking and ready to escape! Then the Lord spoke to me again telling me I had done it. I didn't understand what the Lord was getting at - I had taken the word forward, but that wasn't what the Lord was saying. What I had done was walked through crowds of people; I had faced my fear.

I sat down and words started to flow. For the first time ever my feelings started being released and I started writing. Throughout 2014 & 2015 words continued to come and at New Wine 2015 the book was completed. I had been struggling with a title and again the Lord showed me the words to use. For years I had been trying to break free from circumstances and feelings —° 'Breaking Free' was to be the title of the book.

I pray that as you read the words in these verses that the Lord will speak to you as He did to me and that you will find comfort and peace in releasing your feelings.

The Tree

I look to the cross and what do I see
I see a man nailed to a tree
A man who died to give me life
Who made the ultimate sacrifice

He died to set me free
So that I'm not nailed upon that tree
He took my burdens, laid them down
Then on me he put a crown

He is transforming me from the inside out
He helped me learn to sing and shout
To give glory to the Father and praise to the Son
To live with the Spirit, so I've no need to run

He changed my life, He set me free
I know I'm not upon that tree
I am transformed, I am renewed
With Jesus is the life I choose

For with God there is no doubt
For He knows me inside out
I'm loved, I'm cherished, and I'm a Holy Bride
Now in me there is no pride

He see's me and He knows me
He loves me all the same
In Him there is no doubt
In Him I have no shame

So when you look upon that tree
You'll see the man who set you free
You'll see the man who gave you life
Who paid the ultimate sacrifice

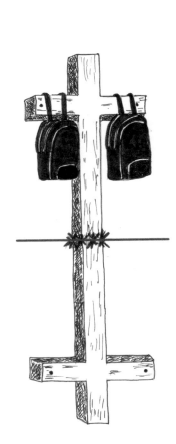

Where Can I Run

Where can I run to, where can I hide
Where can I go, where God can't find
Into the depths of despair I will go
Hoping no one can see, no one can know

I'll put on the mask, put on the face
Say "I'm alright, I'm fine, it's ok"
But I can't run from God, from Him I cannot hide
He's always with me, always at my side

He never leaves me, I'm never alone
No matter the problem, what ever's at home
When panic arises escape I must find
But God is there with me, the help He provides

The Spirit indwells to comfort me there
The friend alongside to hug and to care
The prayer that is said, the words that will bless
They lift the despair and then there is rest

From God there's no hiding, no escape can be found
He's right there beside you, with Him you are bound

Love

There is excitement to be found here
There is joy in this place
The finding of Jesus
The finding of Grace

The soaking of the Spirit
The justice of the Lord
All can be found here
All this and more

Allow Him to work within you
Work within your life
To bring you peace and love and joy
To take from you your strife

Let His waters flood you
Let Him take your pain
Let Him wash over you afresh
Let His love flow in you again

Do We

Do we celebrate, do we give our lives
Do we make the ultimate sacrifice
Live for God as He lives for us
Give our lives without a fuss

Or do we hold onto the past
Feel too old, think life's gone by
Wonder why we should even try

God never gives up on us
He never leaves us alone
He has a place for us by His throne

We have life so let's celebrate
Give glory to the living Lord, dance and shout
This is what life is all about

Arms of Love

God knew me and He loved me
Before the world began
For I know my name is written
In the palm of God's right hand

He holds me when I tremble
He knows when I'm afraid
His love He wraps around me
And in His arms I lay

By the power of His Spirit
He works within my life
He teaches me forgiveness
And how to cope with strife

For God gave His Son to save me
To take my sin away
To build me up and help me
To live from day to day

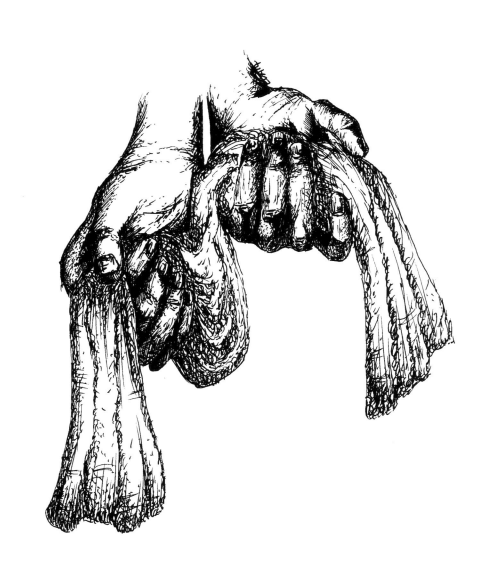

Jesus

Jesus is our Saviour, Jesus is our King
Let's not forget a single thing

He teaches us to love each other, He teaches us to serve
To help and encourage with a single word

Let's give our lives to Jesus
Let's let the Spirit in
For He's the one to heal us
To save us from our sin

Jesus is our Saviour, Jesus is our King

Plans

Thank you Lord for loving me
Just the way I am
For not judging or condemning me
As I follow my own plan

Although you give me guidance
Show me how to live my life
I sometimes chose the world to follow
Turn and look back just like Lots wife

I choose to go against your word
To search for my own path
To find my way upon this earth
Not worried about your wrath

Although you sent your Son Lord
To save me from my sin
I still live life my own way
Not letting you in

And yet Lord you still love me
You still want me to follow you
To live my life with a purpose
To follow all things through

You wait patiently for me Lord
To choose which path to go
To decide the life I want to lead
Help me Lord to know

Know when to stop and listen
To the words you've given me
To show the right path to follow
So you Lord I can always see

Thank you Lord for loving me
Just the way I am
For not judging or condemning me
As I try to follow Lord your plan

Come

Come into this place Lord
Come and fill our souls
Pour your love upon us
Let us overflow
With the power of your Spirit
With your fire burning bright
Let your Glory shine in us
Let us be your light

In a world that's full of darkness
In a world that's full of pain
How Lord can we hope
How can we hide our shame
How can we walk forward
Hold our heads up high
Learn to trust in you Lord
To listen and abide

In Jesus we have a Saviour
Who took from us our sin
We have no need to run and hide
We need to let Him in
To pray to God the Father
To read and learn God's word
To meditate with the Spirit
So His voice can be heard

To love and serve all others
To show Jesus Christ in us
To let the light shine from our hearts
And let His word impart
Impart from deep within us
To our family and our friends
To spread the gospel further
So our journey never ends

Come into this place Lord
Come and fill our souls
Pour your love upon us
Let us overflow
With the power of your Spirit
With your fire burning bright
Let your Glory shine in us
Let us be your light

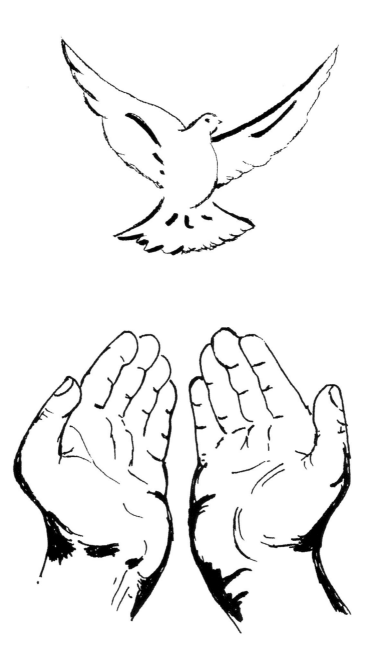

Prayer

Lord when I pray
How do I know
That the words I am sayingWhere will they go

Will they go to heaven
Will you hear them there
Will you understand
What I'm trying to share

Will my words be enough
For you to intercede
For the power of your Spirit
To guide and to lead

Lord help me to trust you
Lord help me to know
That the prayer I am saying
To you it will go

Lord let my prayer
Just be the start
Let me speak clearly
Straight from the heart

Let me not worry
About what I should say
Let me give myself completely
To you as I pray

Words

Thank you Lord, for giving us
The power of your word
To help us and to guide us
When we are so perturbed

By what's going on around us
In this world in which we live
A world that's full of fear and pain
Where something has to give

Help us give our lives to you
To learn to trust in you
To find the peace around us
Which only you can do

The bible is our handbook
Your Spirit is our guide
The help is there before us
The words that you provide

To show us the way forward
And how to live our lives
To learn to love and trust and give
For this is what we strive

Thank you Lord for giving us
The power of your word
To help us and to guide us
When we are so perturbed

Wonder

Did you laugh, did you cry
Did you ever wonder why
You had to live and then to die
In such a cruel way

Did you ever question
What your Father said
Did you ever doubt
The places you were led

Did your love for your Father
Cloud where you should go
Or did the thoughts in your mind
Make you really low

Help us to know Lord
Help us to understand
How you lived amongst us
How your life was planned

How you suffered for us
How your emotions helped you through
How you lived your life Lord Jesus
As only you could do

You are the resurrection
You are the giver of new life
You gave us our emotions
To help us in our strife

Why

Why do we do it
Why do we turn away
Why do we feel that
We need to make God pay

For all of our troubles
For all of the strife
For all of the bad things
That happen in our life

We don't think God will notice
We don't think God will care
Our lives they are not worthy
There is no need for prayer

Even if we turn to Him
We're sure that He won't hear
We've put Him in a little box
Our plans are not so clear

But we need to know God loves us
We need to know He cares
He won't ever leave us
He'll listen to our prayers

He'll be there beside us
With every step we take
He won't leave us or forsake us
But the right choice we should make

He didn't cause the problems
He didn't cause our pain
We managed that ourselves
When we let sin enter in

God gave His Son to save us
To come and set us free
He loves us and He helps us
If we let Him be

Be the hope within our Spirit
And the peace within our heart
The saving grace that loves us
Lord help us not depart

Depart Lord from your presence
When fear is in our way
Help us learn to trust you
Every single day

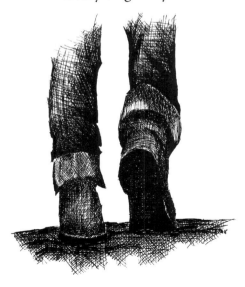

The Pit

Lord why don't we think you'll notice
When we turn our backs on you
When we think our life is over
When there's nothing left to do

We find ourselves snowed under
In a pit with no way out
Our life just feels so empty
We can't even scream or shout

We hide our feelings in a box
A mask upon our face
We won't let anyone enter in
For us there is no grace

We have no way to pull ourselves
Out from that pit of despair
We feel no one can help us
There is no one to care

How very wrong we are Lord
To turn our backs on you
In despair we need to call out
Only you can pull us through

For in you there is salvation
In you we can find peace
As well as grace and hope and love
Our minds can find release

No Mans Land

They gave their lives on battlefields
In a country far away
They had to cross through 'No Mans Land'
And there their bodies lay

There was no class distinction
To those who gave their lives
His Lordship and his servant
They fought side by side

They never really stood a chance
Going 'over the top' that day
Mown down by the enemies guns
In that country far away

With chaos all around them
They must have been afraid
But still they kept on going
And with their lives they paid

So many of them died that day
The fields were red with blood
Yet still they kept on fighting
Walking through the mud

Onwards they kept going
With shooting all around
Did it make a difference
Them capturing that ground

The fields are red again today
But not with soldiers blood
The poppies line up side by side
Where once the soldiers stood

The poppy is the symbol
Of those who gave their life
So that we'll remember
Their ultimate sacrifice

The sacrifice that soldiers make
For freedom in this land
Still goes on each and every day
So with them we must stand

We pray to God that peace will come
And reign upon this earth
To cease the fighting going on
And bring to life new birth

Memories Are Made

Thoughts of the heart
Laughter and tears
Memories are made
The release of our fears

The days gone by
With loved ones and friends
The love that surrounds us
It never ends

The promise of God
Is still in our hearts
Our life doesn't end
When our loved ones depart

Although they've gone home
Not here on this earth
The memories are left
The laughter and mirth

The stories we tell
The memories we share
They're part of our life
We will always care

They might not be with us
To hug and to love
But they've left part of themselves
To descend like a dove

When we're feeling down
When we're feeling low
God gives us the memories
To help us to know

Our loved ones are with us
Always in our heart
They will never leave us
They will never depart

Mum

Determination

Can we make it on our own
Without Jesus in our life
Can we live this life with purpose
Can we handle all the strife

Can we achieve all that Gods given us
The tasks we need to do
To live this life with purpose
To follow all things through

In our own determination
Can we make things right
Do we have the purpose
The vision and the sight

We need the Lord to help us
We need Him to be our strength
To guide us and to fill us
With every living breath

We need Jesus as our Saviour
To stand here by our side
To show us the way forward
To help remove our pride

Without His Holy presence
Being central in our life
We can't achieve all God's given
We can't handle all the strife

Lord you alone can help us
Help us to succeed
To use the gifts you've given us
To further spread your seed

Into the lives of others
Who you place upon our heart
Help us learn to love them
Your wisdom to depart

We need determination
In all the things we do
But without the love of Jesus
We just can't follow through

Inspiration

Lord you are my inspiration
Lord you are my song
Lord you are the help I need
When things in life go wrong

You are the one who picks me up
Who floods my life with peace
With joy and love and laughter
Your wonders never cease

Lord without you in my life
The whole world looks so blue
The burdens build upon me
I don't know what to do

The weight upon my shoulders
It starts to bring me down
If only I would turn to you
You'd put on me a crown

So Lord I give my life to you
Lord I give my heart
Each day you draw me closer
Lord help me not depart

Depart Lord from your presence
From all you've given me
You gave your life to save me
You died so I'd be free

So Lord help me to love you
With all that's in my soul
To keep my eyes upon you
Lord you make me whole

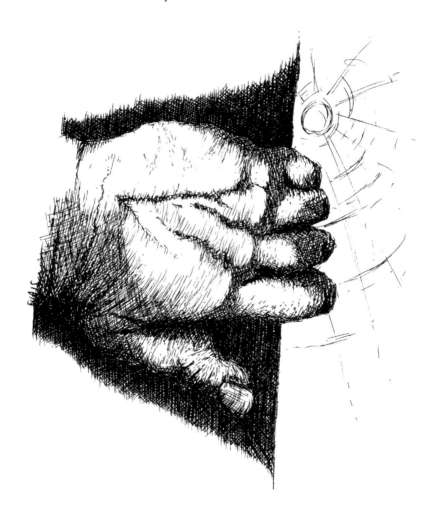

Life

What is the life you've given us
What are we to do
How are we to live
A life that pleases you

Lord you're our salvation
You died that we might live
You're the one to follow
Our lives to you we give

Help us learn to trust you
To follow not to doubt
To give our lives in service
To turn ourselves about

Help us not to worry
What other people think
To live our lives in freedom
From God's cup to drink

Lord we are your servants
We want to follow you
To learn to serve and love and give
Is what we want to do

Lord you're our salvation
Of that there is no doubt
Lord help us to trust you
To turn our lives about

Creation

What is creation
If it's not about life
What are we here for
Why the trouble and strife

If God didn't create us
Then why are we here
What's life about
Is there reason to cheer

Is there a purpose
Without God in our heart
Or are we just living
Waiting for time to depart

What is the point
Of living a good life
If we have no hope in Jesus
Where's redemption for our strife

If we live our lives
With no thought for others
Then what is the point
Why do we bother

But God created each of us
Our life He has planned
He created the earth
He created this land

He created the birds
And the fish in the sea
He created the mountains
As well as you and me

Jesus is our salvation
In Him our hope and grace
Let's give our lives to Jesus
Let Him help us run the race

Whirlwind

My mind is like a whirlwind
Going round and round
Not even in the centre
Can any peace be found

If it's not "What is for dinner?"
Or "What's the meeting for tonight?"
"How can I fit in the hairdressers?"
Or "Do our finances add up right?"

Then there's worry over children
Or maybe it's our health
Should we see the Dr
Or worry over our wealth

The world in which we live
Bombards us from every side
The TV with its adverts
Advising everything can be tried

From pills to help our bodies
To foods that help loose weight
To toning with no exercise
And finding our soul mate

The magazines all tell us
How we should live our life
There's horoscopes for day to day
And reading of others strife

If we buy the winning ticket
Then our life will be a dream
With no financial worries
We'll be the cat that got the cream

And then we place our value
On what other people think
We try to keep up with the Joneses
And that's when we start to sink

We have to have that flat screen
And maybe that new car
We need to have that holiday
We've worked too hard by far

How can we keep on going
Living life at such a pace
It just doesn't get any easier
We are always in a race

A race to get things finished
Before the TV program starts
When we can sit down for a minute
But from the chair we don't depart

We have our evening dinner
Sat in front of the TV
Our minds not concentrating
On anything we see

We know we should make the effort
To spend some time in prayer
But that means moving from the sofa
We're sure God won't really care

But without God in the centre
Of each and every day
How can we find the peace
To make the whirlwind go away

God gives our lives a purpose
The Holy Spirit is our guide
Jesus is our salvation
He's always on our side

In God we find the answer
Of how we should live our lives
By giving Him our burdens
Our worry and our strife

God won't ever condemn us
Or judge the things we do
He'll love us and He'll help us
As we keep on muddling through

So be still and sit in His presence
Let God be your refuge and strength
Let Him drive out the fear and the worry
Let His peace be your every breath

My Lord

You're my Lord and my redeemer
You're my helper and my friend
In this world that's full of trouble
You're with me to the end

You made the heavens high above me
You made the earth on which I live
You are mightier than the oceans
And yet to me your peace you give

Your protections all around me
You're the shade at my right hand
Through the day the sun wont harm me
On my life no vengeance planned

You're my Lord and my redeemer
You're my helper and my friend
In this world that's full of trouble
You're with me to the end

What is Life

What is life without you Lord
Life is a living hell
A separation from the one I love
Not knowing where I dwell

What is life without you Lord
It's a roaming every day
Not knowing where I'm going
Not knowing where I'll stay

What is the life you've given me
The sacrifice you gave
To give me joy and peace and love
To know now where I stay

What is the life you've given me
A sacrifice for my sin
You've given me the chance to live
You've made me whole again

You've bridged the separation
By the giving of your life
You've made me one with you again
Within you there's no strife

I've found the joy and love and peace
That you have given me
And I thank you Lord for loving me
And dying on that tree